1957 U.S. YEARBOOK

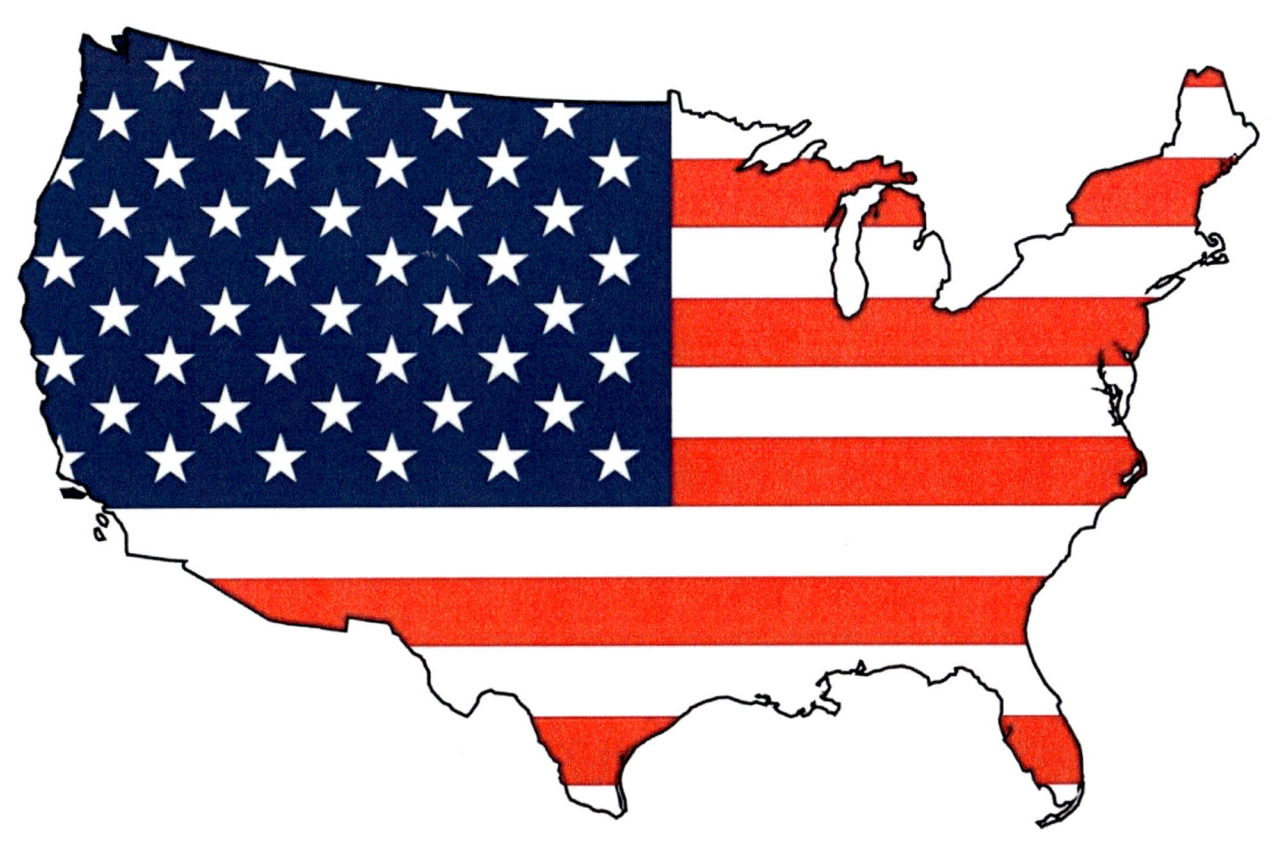

© Liberty Eagle Publishing Ltd. 2016
All Rights Reserved
ISBN-10: 1533556040
ISBN-13: 978-1533556042

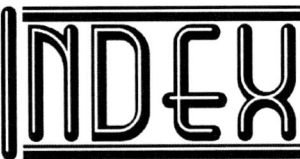

People In High Office	Page 4
Events	Page 8
Births - U.S. Personalities	Page 14
Music - Top 10 Singles	Page 19
Films - Top 5 Films	Page 25
Sporting Winners	Page 41
Cost Of Living	Page 50

FIRST EDITION

People In High Office

President: Dwight D. Eisenhower
Republican Party
January 20, 1953 - January 20, 1961

Born October 14, 1890 Eisenhower was a former 5 star general in the U.S. Army during WWII and the first Supreme Commander of NATO. He served as the 34th President of the United States and died January 22, 1973.

48 stars (1912-1959)

Vice President: Richard Nixon
Chief Justice: Earl Warren
Speaker of the House of Representatives: Sam Rayburn
Senate Majority Leader: Lyndon B. Johnson

United Kingdom

Prime Ministers
Sir Anthony Eden - Conservative Party
6th April 1955 - 10th January 1957
Harold Macmillan - Conservative Party
10th January 1957 - 19th October 1963

Monarch:
Queen Elizabeth II

Rest Of The World

Australia

Prime Minister
Sir Robert Menzies

Brazil

President
Juscelino Kubitschek

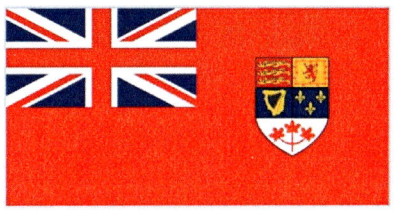

Canada

Prime Ministers
Louis St. Laurent
John Diefenbaker

China

Chairman
Mao Zedong

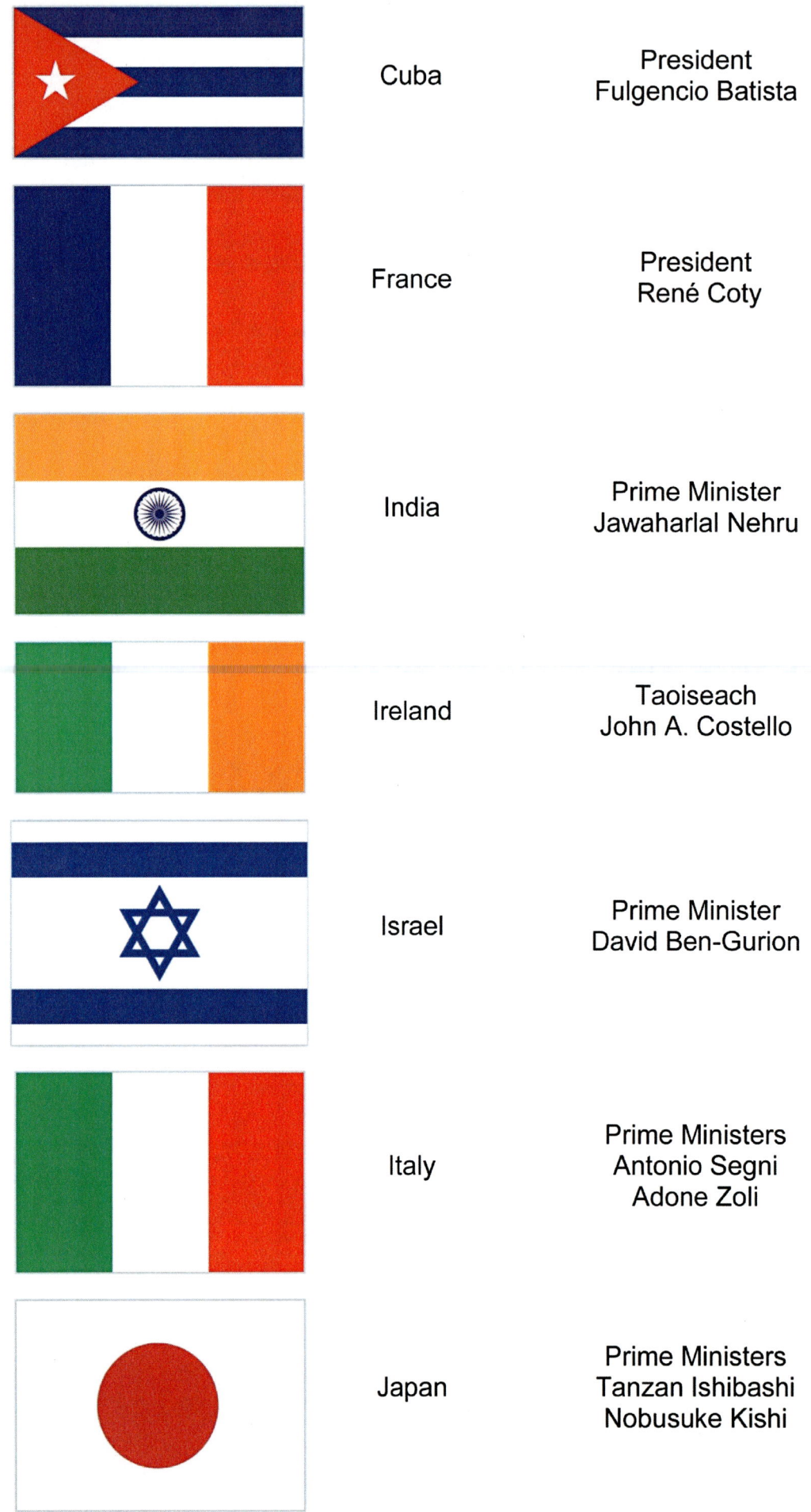

Cuba	President Fulgencio Batista
France	President René Coty
India	Prime Minister Jawaharlal Nehru
Ireland	Taoiseach John A. Costello
Israel	Prime Minister David Ben-Gurion
Italy	Prime Ministers Antonio Segni / Adone Zoli
Japan	Prime Ministers Tanzan Ishibashi / Nobusuke Kishi

 Mexico — President Adolfo Ruiz Cortines

 New Zealand — Prime Ministers Sidney Holland, Keith Holyoake, Walter Nash

 Pakistan — Prime Ministers Huseyn Shaheed Suhrawardy, Ibrahim Ismail Chundrigar, Feroz Khan Noon

 South Africa — Prime Minister Johannes Gerhardus Strijdom

 Spain — President Francisco Franco

 Soviet Union — Communist Party Leader Nikita Khrushchev

 West Germany — Chancellor Konrad Adenauer

EVENTS FROM 1957

JANUARY

2   The San Francisco and Los Angeles stock exchanges merge to form the Pacific Coast Stock Exchange.

6   Elvis Presley appears on The Ed Sullivan Show for the third and final time. Elvis' appearance on the show contains the legendary moments when the CBS censors would not allow his entire body to be shown. Seen only from the waist up, Elvis still put on an exciting show singing seven songs in three segments. Describing Elvis Ed Sullivan said; "This is a real decent, fine boy. We've never had a pleasanter experience on our show with a big name than we've had with you. You're thoroughly alright."

20   Dwight D. Eisenhower is inaugurated for a second term as President of the United States.

22   The New York City "Mad Bomber", George P. Metesky, is arrested in Waterbury, Connecticut and is charged with planting more than 30 bombs.

23   Ku Klux Klan members force truck driver Willie Edwards to jump off a bridge into the Alabama River (he drowns as a result).

31   Pacoima aircraft accident: Three students on a junior high school playground in Pacoima, California are among the 8 people killed following a mid-air collision between a Douglas DC-7 airliner and a Northrop F-89 Scorpion fighter jet in the skies above the San Fernando Valley section of Los Angeles.

FEBRUARY

February 4, 1957: The first nuclear-powered submarine, the USS Nautilus (SSN-571), logs its 60,000th nautical mile matching the endurance of the fictional Nautilus described in Jules Verne's novel Twenty Thousand Leagues Under the Sea. (Pictured New York 1956)

FEBRUARY

- 17 — The Warrenton Nursing Home Fire kills 72 people.
- 25 — The Boy In The Box is discovered along a sidewalk in Philadelphia. The murder victim is described as Caucasian in appearance and 4 to 6 years old. The case is never solved.

MARCH

- 7 — The United States Congress approves the Eisenhower Doctrine.
- 10 — Floodgates of The Dalles Dam are closed inundating Celilo Falls and ancient Indian fisheries along the Columbia River in Oregon.
- 13 — The United States Federal Bureau of Investigation arrests Jimmy Hoffa and charges him with bribery.
- 25 — 22-year-old Elvis Presley buys Graceland on 3734 Bellevue Boulevard (Highway 51 South) for $102,500. He and his family move from their house on 1034 Audubon Drive which Elvis had bought only a year earlier.
- 27 — The 29th Academy Awards ceremony is held.
- 31 — Rodgers and Hammerstein's Cinderella, the team's only musical written especially for television, is telecast live and in color by CBS. Starring Julie Andrews in the title role the production is seen by millions. This version is not telecast again for more than 40 years.

Elvis Presley Buys $100,000 Home

MEMPHIS, Tenn., March 23 (INS) —Rock and rolling Elvis Presley became a country squire today, purchasing a $100,000 country residence for himself and his parents.

The 22-year-old guitar strummer said he was swapping in his present smaller Memphis home as part payment on the modern two-story five-bedroom establishment.

The new home, boasting a four-car garage, is located on a 13½ acre tract of land in Whitehaven south of Memphis near the Mississippi state line.

The property is adjacent to a church. When notified of the sale, pastor Howard Stevens said he was "pleased" to have the controversial pelvis pulsating singer as a neighbor.

Construction of Graceland began in 1939 by Dr. & Mrs Thomas Moore and was named after Mrs Moore's Aunt Grace Toof who was the original landowner. Elvis' Parents and grandmother moved in on May 16 but Elvis did not spend his first night there until June 26, 1957 due to filming Jailhouse Rock.

APRIL

- 12 — 520 copies of Allen Ginsberg's poem Howl, imported from London, are seized by U.S. customs officials on the grounds of obscenity.

MAY

2   Vincent Gigante fails to assassinate mafioso Frank Costello in Manhattan.

3   Brooklyn Dodgers owner Walter O'Malley agrees to move the team from Brooklyn, New York to Los Angeles.

JUNE

15   Oklahoma celebrates its semi-centennial statehood by burying a brand new 1957 Plymouth Belvedere in a time capsule (to be opened 50 years later).

20   The 1957 Fargo Tornado starts at 7:30pm. It causes $25.8 million in damages (the equivalent of $218 million today) and kills 10. This tornado is considered the most devastating in North Dakota history and is one of only two F5 tornadoes that have struck the state (the other was 4 years earlier in 1953).

25   The United Church of Christ is formed in Cleveland, Ohio by the merger of the Congregational Christian Churches and the Evangelical and Reformed Church.

27   Hurricane Audrey demolishes Cameron, Louisiana, killing 400 people.

The Oklahoma Plymouth Belvedere being buried in 1957 and being recovered in 2007.

Residents of Tulsa, Oklahoma were enjoying their state's anniversary in a party called "Tulsarama!" when Tulsa representatives decided they needed something unique to compete with other cities. They decided to entomb an automobile in a time capsule using a 1957 Plymouth Belvedere. During the party residents were asked to guess the population of Tulsa in 2007. The guesses were sealed in a steel container and placed in the car. The winner or their heir would receive the Plymouth and a $100 trust fund. Unfortunately, when recovered, it wasn't quite in the same pristine shape it was when it was buried. It was discovered that it had been wading under 4 feet of water for some time. The rather rusty vehicle was awarded to Bowling Green resident Catherine Johnson who was the closest relative to Ray Humbertson who had predicted the city's population most accurately. The $100 trust fund had reportedly increased to $400.

JULY

9   Elvis Presley's Loving You opens in theatres.

16   United States Marine Major John Glenn flies an F8U supersonic jet from California to New York in 3 hours, 23 minutes and 8 seconds, setting a new transcontinental speed record.

AUGUST

5	American Bandstand, a local dance show produced by WFIL-TV in Philadelphia, joins the ABC Television Network.
21	President Dwight D. Eisenhower announces a 2-year suspension of nuclear testing.
28	United States Senator Strom Thurmond (D-SC) sets the record for the longest filibuster with his 24h 18min speech against the civil rights bill.

SEPTEMBER

4	American Civil Rights Movement - Little Rock Crisis: Governor Orville Faubus of Arkansas calls out the U.S. National Guard to prevent African-American students from enrolling in Central High School in Little Rock.
4	The Ford Motor Company introduces the Edsel on what the company proclaims as "E Day".
9	The Catholic Memorial High School opens its doors for the first time in Boston, Massachusetts.
24	President Dwight D. Eisenhower sends federal troops to Arkansas to provide safe passage into Central High School for the Little Rock Nine.
26	West Side Story, a new musical by Leonard Bernstein, Jerome Robbins, Arthur Laurents and Stephen Sondheim opens at the Winter Garden Theatre on Broadway.

West Side Story, set in 1950s New York City, was inspired by Romeo and Juliet. The 1957 Broadway production ran for 732 performances before going on tour.

OCTOBER

9	Neil H. McElroy is sworn in as United States Secretary of Defense.
10	President Dwight D. Eisenhower apologizes to the finance minister of Ghana, Komla Agbeli Gbdemah, after he is refused service in a Dover, Delaware restaurant.
11	The orbit of the last stage of the R-7 Semyorka rocket (carrying Sputnik I) is first successfully calculated on an IBM 704 computer by teams at The M.I.T. Computation Center and Operation Moonwatch in Cambridge, Massachusetts.
21	Army Capt. Hank Cramer of the 1st Special Forces Group becomes the U.S. military's first combat fatality in Vietnam.
25	Mafia boss Albert Anastasia is assassinated in a barber shop at the Park Sheraton Hotel in New York City.
31	Toyota starts exporting vehicles to the U.S. beginning with the Toyota Crown and the Toyota Land Cruiser

NOVEMBER

November 1, 1957: The Mackinac Bridge, the world's longest suspension bridge between anchorages at the time and connecting Michigan's two peninsulas, opens to traffic. At the grand opening 83 beauty queens, representing all the counties in Michigan, crossed the Mackinac Bridge in Oldsmobile Convertibles. Familiarly known as Big Mac and Mighty Mac, the bridge was designed by engineer David B. Steinman and is 26,372 feet long.

6	Jailhouse Rock opens nationally and Elvis Presley continues to gain more notoriety.
7	Cold War: In the United States the Gaither Report calls for more American missiles and fallout shelters.
14	Apalachin Meeting: American Mafia leaders meet in Apalachin, New York at the house of Joseph Barbara. An estimated 100 Mafiosi members from the United States, Italy and Cuba are thought to have been at this meeting.
16	Edward Gein murders his last victim, Bernice Worden of Plainfield, Wisconsin.
16	Oklahoma celebrates its 50th anniversary of statehood.

NOVEMBER

16	Notre Dame beats Oklahoma 7-0 ending the Sooners' 47-game, 1,512-day college football winning streak. The game also marked the first time in more than 120 games that Oklahoma didn't score a single point.
25	President Dwight D. Eisenhower suffers a stroke.

DECEMBER

2	Shippingport Atomic Power Station goes online with commercial operations beginning on May 26, 1958.
6	Vanguard TV3 becomes the first U.S. attempt to launch a satellite. It fails with the rocket blowing up on the launch pad.
19	Meredith Willson's classic musical, The Music Man starring Robert Preston, debuts on Broadway.
20	A Boeing 707 airliner flies for the first time.
22	The CBS afternoon anthology series, Seven Lively Arts, presents Tchaikovsky's ballet The Nutcracker on U.S. television for the first time.

Vanguard Test Vehicle Three was the first U.S. attempt to launch a satellite into orbit around the Earth. At its launch at Cape Canaveral the booster ignited and began to rise but about two seconds after lift-off, after rising about four feet, the rocket lost thrust and began to fall back to the launch pad. As it settled the fuel tanks ruptured and exploded, destroying the rocket and severely damaging the launch pad. The Vanguard satellite was thrown clear and landed on the ground a short distance away with its transmitters still sending out a beacon signal. Newspapers across the United States published prominent headlines and articles noting the failure including plays on the name of the Russian satellite, Sputnik, such as "Flopnik", "Kaputnik", "Oopsnik" and "Stayputnik".

UNDATED EVENTS FROM 1957

The Civil Rights Commission is established in the USA under the Civil Rights Act of 1957.

US Personalities Born in 1957

Patty Loveless
January 4, 1957

Country music singer born Patty Lee Ramey. Since her emergence in late 1986 with her first (self-titled) album, Loveless has been one of the most popular female singers of the neo traditional country movement. To date, Loveless has charted more than 40 singles on the Billboard Hot Country Songs charts included five No.1's. Additionally she has recorded 14 studio albums in the U.S. with four of these having been certified platinum and two certified gold.

Nancy Marie Lopez
January 6, 1957

Professional golfer who became a member of the LPGA Tour in 1977 and won 48 LPGA Tour events including three major championships. Although considered one of the greats in the history of women's golf, and the best player from the late 1970s to late 1980s, Lopez did not win many majors and never won the U.S. Women's Open (she finished second four times). Lopez was inducted into the World Golf Hall of Fame in 1987.

Katherine Anne "Katie" Couric
January 7, 1957

Journalist and author who currently serves as Yahoo! Global News Anchor. Couric has been a television host on all Big Three television networks in the U.S. working for NBC News from 1989 to 2006, CBS News from 2006 to 2011 and ABC News from 2011 to 2014. As an author Couric's first book, The Best Advice I Ever Got: Lessons from Extraordinary Lives, was a New York Times best-seller. In 2004 Couric was inducted into the Television Hall of Fame.

Broderick Stephen Harvey
January 17, 1957

Comedian, television host, radio personality, actor and author known professionally Steve Harvey. He hosts The Steve Harvey Morning Show, Steve Harvey (the talk show), Family Feud and Little Big Shots. He is also the author of Act Like a Lady, Think Like a Man, which was published in March 2009 and the book Straight Talk, No Chaser: How to Find and Keep a Man. Harvey is a three-time Daytime Emmy Award winner and a 13-time NAACP Image Award winner in various categories.

Ottis Jerome "O.J." Anderson
January 19, 1957

Former American Football running back. In 1979 Anderson had what was probably the greatest debut game in NFL history with the St. Louis Cardinals when he rushed for 193 yards. Later that year he was named the NFL Offensive Rookie of the Year by the Associated Press. In 1991 he was named the MVP of Super Bowl XXV when playing with the New York Giants. Anderson is one of just 29 running backs in the history of the NFL to rush for more than 10,000 yards.

William Payne Stewart
January 30, 1957 - October 25, 1999

Professional golfer who won eleven PGA Tour events, including three major championships, the last of which occurred a few months before he died in an airplane accident at the age of 42. Stewart was a popular golfer with spectators who responded enthusiastically to his distinctive clothing. He was reputed to have the biggest wardrobe of all professional golfers and was a favorite of photographers because of his flamboyant attire of ivy caps and patterned pants.

Shirley Frances Babashoff
January 31, 1957

Former competition swimmer, Olympic champion and former world record-holder in multiple events. Babashoff set six world records and won a total of eight individual Olympic medals in her career. She won a gold medal in the 400-meter freestyle relay in both the 1972 and 1976 Olympics as well as winning gold in the 1975 World Championships in both the 200-meter and 400-meter freestyle. During her career she set 37 national records and at one stage held all national freestyle records in the 100-meter to 800-meter events.

Jimmy Spencer
February 15, 1957

Former television commentator and NASCAR driver. Spencer hosted the NASCAR-inspired talk show, What's the Deal? and was co-host with John Roberts and Kenny Wallace of Speed's pre-race and post-race NASCAR shows NASCAR RaceDay and NASCAR Victory Lane. During his days racing 'modifieds', he was nicknamed "Mr. Excitement" for his aggressive racing style. Spencer is one of the few drivers to have won a race in all three of NASCAR's top series: Sprint Cup, Xfinity and the Camping World Truck Series.

Levardis Robert Martyn Burton, Jr.
February 16, 1957

Actor, presenter, director and author. Professionally known as LeVar Burton his most successful roles have been as the young Kunta Kinte in the 1977 award-winning ABC television mini-series Roots, Lt. Commander Geordi La Forge in Star Trek: The Next Generation and as the host of the long-running PBS children's series Reading Rainbow. Burton is on the board of directors for the Directors Guild of America and for the AIDS Research Alliance (a not for profit research organization dedicated to finding a cure for AIDS).

Cynthia Leigh "Cindy" Wilson
February 28, 1957

Vocalist, songwriter and a founding member of new wave rock band The B-52s. Their 1979 debut album, The B-52's, yielded the hit singles "Rock Lobster" and "Planet Claire" and launched the band into stardom. The B-52s most recent album Funplex (2008) reached No.11 on the U.S. Billboard 200 with Wilson co-writing every song on the album with the other band members. Summer 2015 saw the band touring with Tears for Fears, The English Beat and The Psychedelic Furs.

Vincent Grant "Vince" Gill
April 12, 1957

Country singer, songwriter and multi-instrumentalist who has achieved commercial success and fame both as frontman to the country rock band Pure Prairie League in the 1970s and as a solo artist since 1983. Gill has recorded more than 20 studio albums, charted over 40 singles and has sold more than 26 million albums. He has received 18 CMA Awards by the Country Music Association and earned 20 Grammy Awards (a record for a male country artist). In 2007 he was inducted into the Country Music Hall of Fame.

Evelyn Ashford
April 15, 1957

Retired track and field athlete, Ashford won four Olympic gold medals including the 100-meter dash (Los Angeles 1984) and the 4x100m relay (Los Angeles 1984, Seoul 1988 and Barcelona 1992). She ran under the 11-second barrier over 30 times, was the first to run under 11 seconds at an Olympic Games and is the oldest woman to win an Olympic gold medal in track and field. In 1997 Ashford was inducted into the National Track and Field Hall of Fame where she is said to be "one of the greatest track and field runners ever."

Dominic Lee Pudwill Gorie
May 2, 1957

Retired United States Navy officer and NASA astronaut. Gorie is a veteran of four space shuttle missions and flew 38 combat missions during Operation Desert Storm in the first Gulf War. During his career he has been awarded the Defense Meritorious Service Medal, the Legion of Merit, 2 Distinguished Flying Crosses (one with a Combat V), 2 Air Medals, the Defense Superior Service Medal, 3 NASA Space Flight Medals and 2 Navy Commendation Medals with Combat V's.

Louis Rodman Whitaker, Jr.
May 12, 1957

Former Major League Baseball player, nicknamed "Sweet Lou", Whitaker was a second baseman for the Detroit Tigers from 1977 to 1995. Along with teammate Alan Trammell he was part of the longest running "double play" combination in major league history. Whitaker is a winner of an American League Rookie of the Year Award (1978), is a 5 time All-Star (1983-1985), a World Series Champion (1984) and holder of 3 Gold Glove Awards (1983-1985) and 4 Silver Slugger Awards (1983-1985, 1987).

William "Bill" Laimbeer, Jr.
May 19, 1957

Retired basketball player who spent most of his career with the Detroit Pistons. Playing at center the 6'11" Laimbeer was a four-time NBA All-Star and integral part of the Pistons teams that won back to back NBA Championships in both 1989 and 1990. After his playing career Laimbeer served as the head coach of the WNBA's Detroit Shock (2002-2009), coaching the team to 3 league championships. Since 2013 he has been the head coach New York Liberty of the WNBA.

Edward Ernest "Judge" Reinhold, Jr.
May 21, 1957

Actor probably best known for co-starring in movies such as Beverly Hills Cop, Ruthless People, Fast Times at Ridgemont High, Gremlins and The Santa Clause trilogy. Reinhold was nominated for an Emmy for a role on Seinfeld in which he played the infamous "close talker" who developed an obsession with Jerry's parents. He has also been seen in Steven Spielberg's epic miniseries Into the West and replaced Charles Grodin in two direct-to-video movies in the Beethoven film series.

Lisa Ann Murkowski
May 22, 1957

Senior U.S. Senator from Alaska and a member of the Republican Party who has served in the Senate since 2002. She became the state's senior senator when Ted Stevens lost his election in 2009. When she ran for a second term in 2010 she lost the Republican Party nomination to Tea Party candidate Joe Miller. She then ran as a write-in candidate and defeated both Miller and Democrat Scott McAdams in the general election making her the first senator to be elected by write-in vote since Strom Thurmond in 1954.

Rick Douglas Husband
July 12, 1957 –
February 1, 2003

U.S. Air Force Colonel, pilot and astronaut. Husband served on two Space Shuttle missions; firstly as Pilot on STS-96 in 1999 logging 235 hours and 13 minutes in space and then as Commander of Space Shuttle Columbia mission STS-107. He and the rest of the crew of STS-107 were killed when Columbia disintegrated during re-entry into the Earth's atmosphere. Husband has numerous awards and decorations including the Congressional Space Medal of Honor.

Melanie Griffith
August 9, 1957

Actress who made her credited debut opposite Gene Hackman in Night Moves (1975). She rose to prominence for her role in Brian De Palma's Body Double (1984), which earned her a National Society of Film Critics Award for Best Supporting Actress. Griffith's subsequent performance in Something Wild (1986) garnered critical acclaim before she was cast in Working Girl (1988) which earned her a nomination for the Academy Award for Best Actress and won her a Golden Globe.

Jerry D. Bailey
August 29, 1957

Regarded as one of the world's all-time greatest jockeys, Bailey's mounts have won 5,893 races and $296 million during his 31-year riding career. He won each Triple Crown race twice, scored a record five wins in the Breeders' Cup Classic and notched a record four victories in the Dubai World Cup. Bailey is the only jockey ever to win America's Eclipse Award for Outstanding Jockey seven times including an unprecedented four straight years between 2000 and 2003.

Gloria Estefan
September 1, 1957

Cuban-American singer, songwriter, actress and businesswoman born Gloria María Milagrosa Fajardo García. She started off her career as the leading vocalist in the group called "Miami Latin Boys" which eventually became known as Miami Sound Machine. Through her breakthrough single "Conga" in 1985 she became known worldwide and in the summer of 1988 she and the band got their first number-one hit with the song "Anything For You". Estefan has sold an estimated 100 million records worldwide and has won seven Grammy Awards.

Donny Osmond
December 9, 1957

Singer, actor, dancer, radio personality, and former teen idol. Osmond has also been a talk and game show host, record producer and author. In the mid-1960s he and four of his elder brothers gained fame as the Osmonds. He went solo in the early 1970s covering hits such as "Go Away Little Girl" and "Puppy Love". For over thirty-five years he and younger sister Marie have gained fame as Donny & Marie. In 2009 Osmond won the ninth season of ABC's Dancing with the Stars.

Kevin Edward McHale
December 19, 1957

Retired professional basketball player and Basketball Hall of Fame inductee who played his entire professional career for the Boston Celtics. McHale was a part of what many consider the league's best-ever frontline with small forward Larry Bird and center Robert Parish. The trio of Hall of Famers became known as the "Big Three" and led the Celtics to five NBA Finals appearances and three NBA championships (1981, 1984 and 1986). McHale's number 32 jersey was retired by the Celtics on January 30, 1994.

Raymond Albert "Ray" Romano
December 21, 1957

Actor, stand-up comedian, screenwriter and voice actor. Romano is best known for his role on the sitcom Everybody Loves Raymond (for which he received an Emmy Award) and as the voice of "Manny" in the Ice Age film series. He created and starred in the TNT comedy-drama Men of a Certain Age (2009-2011) and from 2012 to 2015 Romano had a recurring role as Hank Rizzoli, a love interest of Sarah Braverman, in Parenthood.

TOP 10 SINGLES

No.1	Elvis Presley	All Shook Up
No.2	Pat Boone	Love Letters In The Sand
No.3	The Diamonds	Little Darlin'
No.4	Tab Hunter	Young Love
No.5	Jimmy Dorsey	So Rare
No.6	Pat Boone	Don't Forbid Me
No.7	Guy Mitchell	Singing The Blues
No.8	Sonny James	Young Love
No.9	Elvis Presley	Too Much
No.10	Perry Como	Round And Round

 # Elvis Presley
All Shook Up

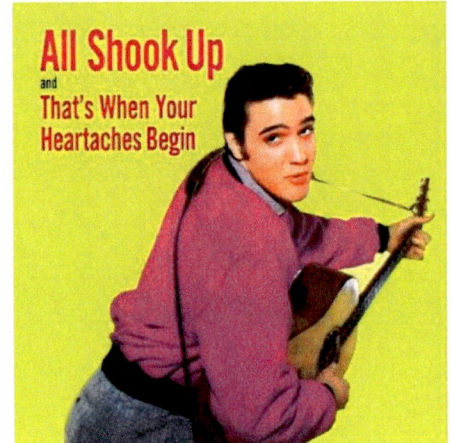  

Label:	Written by:	Length:
RCA	Presley / Blackwell	1 min 57 secs

Elvis Aaron Presley (January 8, 1935 - August 16, 1977) was a singer and actor. Regarded as one of the most significant cultural icons and influential musicians of the 20th century he is often referred to as 'the King of Rock and Roll', or simply, 'the King'. All Shook Up topped the U.S. Billboard Hot 100 on April 13, 1957 staying there for eight weeks. It also topped the Billboard R&B chart for four weeks, becoming Presley's second single to do so, and peaked at No. 3 on the country chart. It is certified 2x Platinum by the RIAA.

 # Pat Boone
Love Letters In The Sand

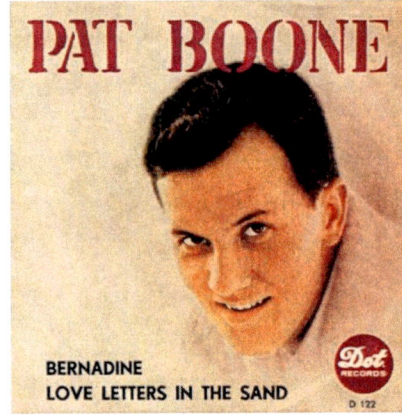  

Label:	Written by:	Length:
Dot Records	C. Kenny / Coots / N. Kenny	2 mins 12 secs

Charles Eugene "Pat" Boone (born June 1, 1934) is a singer, composer, actor, writer, television personality, motivational speaker and spokesman. During the 1950s and early 1960s he sold over 45 million albums, had 38 Top 40 hits and appeared in more than 12 Hollywood films. According to Billboard Boone was the second biggest charting artist of the late 1950s behind only Elvis Presley. Love Letters In The Sand became a major hit in June and July 1957 spending 5 weeks at No.1 on the Billboard Top 100 and 34 weeks in total in the charts.

The Diamonds
Little Darlin'

Label:
Mercury

Written by:
Maurice Williams

Length:
2 mins 5 secs

The Diamonds are a Canadian vocal quartet that rose to prominence in the 1950s and early 1960s with 16 Billboard hit records. The original members were Dave Somerville (lead), Ted Kowalski (tenor), Phil Levitt (baritone) and Bill Reed (bass). They were most noted for interpreting and introducing rhythm and blues vocal group music to the wider pop music audience. The Diamonds' version of Little Darlin' was their biggest selling hit record reaching No.2 on the Billboard Hot 100 and staying there for eight weeks.

Tab Hunter
Young Love

Label:
Dot Records

Written by:
Joyner / Cartey

Length:
2 mins 24 secs

Tab Hunter (born Arthur Andrew Kelm on the July 11, 1931) is an actor, singer and author. Hunter's brief musical career began with the hit single "Young Love" which stayed at No.1 on the Billboard Hot 100 chart for six weeks and sold over one million copies. Under contract to Warner Bros. his success prompted Jack Warner to set up Warner Bros. Records specifically for Hunter.

Jimmy Dorsey
So Rare

Label:
Fraternity Records

Written by:
Jack Sharpe / Jerry Herst

Length:
2 mins 30 secs

James "Jimmy" Dorsey (February 29, 1904 - June 12, 1957) was a prominent jazz clarinettist, saxophonist, composer and big band leader. He recorded and composed the jazz and pop standards "I'm Glad There Is You (In This World Of Ordinary People)" and "It's The Dreamer In Me". So Rare was Dorsey's' final hit record selling over 500,000 copies and staying in the music charts for 26 weeks.

Pat Boone
Don't Forbid Me

Label:
Dot Records

Written by:
Charles Singleton

Length:
2 mins 14 secs

Pat Boone's hit recording of Don't Forbid Me came about after the demo was sent to Elvis Presley's house but had remained there unopened. In Billboard's listing of the Top 100 Top 40 Artists from 1955-1995, Boone was ranked at No.9 and still holds the Billboard record for spending 220 consecutive weeks with at least one song in the charts for each of those weeks. In the 1960s he focused on gospel music and is a member of the Gospel Music Hall of Fame.

Guy Mitchell
Singing The Blues

Label:
Columbia

Written by:
Melvin Endsley

Length:
2 mins 30 secs

Guy Mitchell (born Albert George Cernik, February 22, 1927 - July 1, 1999) was an American pop singer who was not only successful in the U.S. but also the UK and Australia. In total Mitchell sold 44 million records and had six million-selling singles throughout his career. Mitchell's version of Singing The Blues spent ten weeks at No.1 on the U.S. Billboard chart from December 8, 1956 to February 2, 1957. This song was first recorded and released by Marty Robbins in 1956.

Sonny James
Young Love

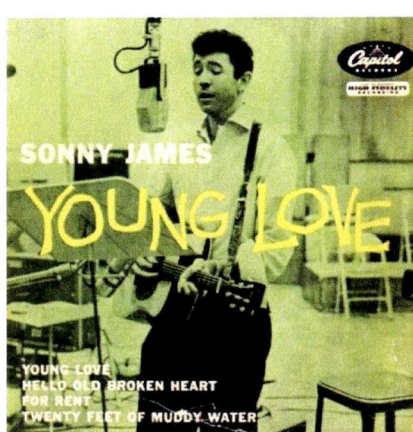

Label:
Capitol Records

Written by:
Carole Joyner / Ric Cartey

Length:
2 mins 29 secs

James Hugh Loden (May 1, 1929 - February 22, 2016) was an American country music singer and songwriter known professionally as Sonny James. His 1957 hit, "Young Love", was probably his most famous song although James did have 72 country and pop charted releases from 1953 to 1983 including an unprecedented five-year streak of 16 straight Billboard No.1 country singles. In total he had 26 No.1 hits and twenty-one of his albums reached the country top ten between 1964 and 1976. James was inducted into the Country Music Hall of Fame in 2007.

Elvis Presley
Too Much

Label:
RCA Victor

Written by:
Bernard Weinman / Lee Rosenberg

Length:
2 mins 30 secs

Elvis Presley recorded Too Much in September 1956 and first performed it on January 6, 1957 on CBS-TV's The Ed Sullivan Show. Commercially successful in many genres, including pop, blues and gospel, Elvis is the best-selling solo artist in the history of recorded music with estimated record sales of around 600 million units worldwide. He won three Grammys and received the Grammy Lifetime Achievement Award at the age of 36.

Perry Como
Round And Round

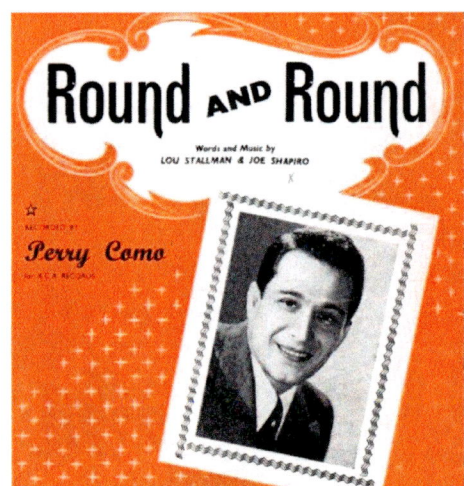

Label:
RCA Victor

Written by:
Joe Shapiro / Lou Stallman

Length:
2 mins 30 secs

Pierino Ronald "Perry" Como (May 18, 1912 - May 12, 2001) was an American singer and television personality. During a career spanning more than half a century he recorded exclusively for RCA Victor after signing with the label in 1943 (44 years in total). Nicknamed "Mr. C.", Como sold millions of records for RCA and pioneered a musical variety television show. The song Round And Round would prove to be Perry Como's last over-all No.1 on the Billboard charts.

TOP FILMS 1957

1. The Bridge On The River Kwai
2. Sayonara
3. Peyton Place
4. Gunfight At The O.K. Corral
5. A Farewell To Arms

OSCARS

Best Film : The Bridge On The River Kwai

Best Director: David Lean
(The Bridge On The River Kwai)
Best Actor: Alec Guinness
(The Bridge On The River Kwai)
Best Actress: Joanne Woodward
(The Three Faces Of Eve)
Best Supporting Actor: Red Buttons
(Sayonara)
Best Supporting Actress: Miyoshi Umeki
(Sayonara)

THE BRIDGE ON THE RIVER KWAI

Directed by: David Lean - Runtime: 161 minutes

After settling his differences with a Japanese PoW camp commander a British colonel co-operates to oversee his men's construction of a railway bridge for their captors while oblivious to a plan by the Allies to destroy it.

Gross $33,300,000

STARRING

William Holden
Born: April 17, 1918
Died: November 12, 1981

Character:
Shears

Actor who was one of the biggest box office draws of the 1950s through the 1970s. Holden won the Academy Award for Best Actor in 1953 for his role in Stalag 17 and a Primetime Emmy Award for Outstanding Lead Actor for his role in the 1973 television film The Blue Knight. The American Film Institute lists Holden as the 25th greatest male star of Classic Hollywood Cinema.

Sir Alec Guinness, CH, CBE
Born: April 2, 1914
Died: August 5, 2000

Character:
Colonel Nicholson

English actor well known for his six collaborations with David Lean including his portrayal of Col. Nicholson in The Bridge on the River Kwai for which he won the Academy Award for Best Actor. Other notable roles include playing Obi-Wan Kenobi in George Lucas's original Star Wars trilogy for which he received a nomination for an Academy Award for Best Supporting Actor.

Jack Hawkins, CBE
Born: September 14, 1910
Died: July 18, 1973

Character:
Major Warden

Actor who worked on stage and in film. Hawkins made his London stage debut aged eleven playing the Elf King in Where the Rainbow Ends (December 1923). During the 1930s he went on to appear in several films but it was only after service in World War II that he began to build a successful career in the cinema. After starring in The Cruel Sea (1953) Hawkins was voted the most popular star in Britain.

TRIVIA

Goofs

The calendar on Colonel Saito's office is correct for February 1943 however the pinup on that calendar was not drawn until 1955 (entitled "Waiting for You" by Gil Elvgren).

During the film Colonel Nicholson reminds Saito that the Geneva Conventions exempt officers from manual labour. In fact Japan was not a signatory of the Geneva Conventions until 1953 therefore there was no expectation by Allied prisoners of being treated in accordance with them.

The movie credits have only one 'n' in Alec Guinness' name (this has been corrected in the "restored" version).

Interesting Facts

At one point during filming David Lean nearly drowned when he was swept away by a river current. Geoffrey Horne saved his life.

CONTINUED

Interesting Facts

The role of Colonel Saito was inspired by Major Risaburo Saito who unlike the character portrayed in the film was said by some to be one of the most reasonable and humane of all of the Japanese officers (usually willing to negotiate with the POWs in return for their labor). Such was the respect between Saito and Lieutenant-Colonel Toosey (the senior Allied officer in the Japanese prisoner-of-war camp at Tha Maa Kham in Thailand during World War II) that Toosey spoke up on Saito's behalf at the war-crimes tribunal after the war saving him from the gallows. Ten years after Toosey's death in 1975 Saito made a pilgrimage to England to visit his grave.

For the scene when Colonel Nicholson emerges from the oven after several days confined there, Alec Guinness based his faltering walk on that of his son Matthew Guinness when he was recovering from polio. Guinness regarded this one tiny scene as some of the finest work he did throughout his entire career.

David Lean initially wanted Nicholson's soldiers to enter the camp while singing "Hitler Has Only Got One Ball", a popular parody of the "Colonel Bogey March" poking fun at Adolf Hitler. Producer Sam Spiegel told him it was too vulgar and the whistling-only version was used instead.

SAYONARA

Directed by: Joshua Logan - Runtime: 147 minutes

A US air force major in Kobe, Japan confronts his own opposition to marriages between American servicemen and Japanese women when he falls for a beautiful performer.

Gross $26,300,000

STARRING

Marlon Brando
Born: April 3, 1924
Died: July 1, 2004

Character:
Major Gruver

Actor, film director and activist. He is credited with bringing a gripping realism to film acting and is often cited as one of the greatest and most influential actors of all time. He helped to popularize the Stanislavski system of acting, today more commonly referred to as method acting. Brando is most famous for his Academy Award-winning performances as Terry Malloy in On the Waterfront (1954) and Vito Corleone in The Godfather (1972).

Patricia Owens
Born: January 17, 1925
Died: August 31, 2000

Character:
Eileen Webster

Owens was a Canadian-born American actress who appeared in about 40 films in a career lasting from 1943 to 1968. At age 18 she made her motion-picture debut in Val Guest's musical comedy Miss London Ltd. Her first American film was Island in the Sun (1957) and Owens' most memorable role was playing Helene Delambre in The Fly (1958) co-starring David Hedison and Vincent Price.

James Garner
Born: April 7, 1928
Died: July 19, 2014

Character:
Captain Bailey

Born James Scott Bumgarner, Garner was an actor, producer, singer, voice artist and comedian. He starred in several television series over more than 5 decades and played leading roles in more than 50 films. Some of his most popular films include The Great Escape (1963), Grand Prix (1966), Victor Victoria (1982), his Academy Award nominated role in Murphy's Romance (1985) and Space Cowboys (2000).

TRIVIA

Goofs

When Major Gruver steps down from the airplane at Kobe airport he is carrying a suitcase and an overcoat but when he approaches General Webster and his wife all his baggage has disappeared.

Major Gruver, said to be a West Point graduate, is shown wearing his class ring on his right hand. Academy graduates always wore their class rings on their left hand as a mark of distinction.

Interesting Facts

According to Turner Classic Movies, Marlon Brando insisted on playing Ace Gruver with a Southern accent against the will of the director Joshua Logan. Logan didn't think that a general's son, who was supposed to be West Point-educated, would speak that way.

Dennis Hopper provided dubbed voices for a few of the smaller characters.

CONTINUED

Interesting Facts

Audrey Hepburn was offered the role of a Japanese bride opposite Marlon Brando but turned it down. She explained; "I couldn't possibly play an Oriental. No one would believe me, they'd laugh. It's a lovely script, however, I know what I can and can't do and if you did persuade me you would regret it because I would be terrible."

Miyoshi Umeki's Academy Award win for Best Supporting Actress, playing Katsumi, made her the first Asian actor to win an Oscar.

The novel Sayonara (1954) follows the romance between Major Gruver and the Japanese woman Hana-Ogi illuminating the racism of the post-WWII time period. Yet by 1956 more than 10,000 American servicemen had defied regulations and married Japanese women (as indeed had the novel's author, James A. Michener).

Marlon Brando was not the first choice for the lead role, it was offered to Rock Hudson but he chose to make A Farewell to Arms (1957) instead.

PEYTON PLACE

Directed by: Mark Robson - Runtime: 157 minutes

Peyton Place is a small fictional New England town where, in the years surrounding World War II, scandal, homicide, suicide, rape and moral hypocrisy hide behind a tranquil façade.

Gross $25,600,000

STARRING

Lana Turner
Born: February 8, 1921
Died: June 29, 1995

Character:
Constance MacKenzie

Film and television actress who was discovered in 1937 and signed by Metro-Goldwyn-Mayer aged just 16. Turner first attracted attention in They Won't Forget (1937) and during the early 1940s she established herself as a leading actress. Her popularity continued during the 1950s with films such as Peyton Place (1957) for which she was nominated for an Academy Award for Best Actress.

Lee Philips
Born: January 10, 1927
Died: March 3, 1999

Character:
Michael Rossi

An actor and television director born in New York City. Philips' acting career started on Broadway and peaked with a starring role as Michael Rossi in this film adaptation of Peyton Place. In the 1960s his career shifted towards directing with credits such as the television series of Peyton Place, The Andy Griffith Show, The Waltons and The Dick Van Dyke Show.

Lloyd Benedict Nolan
Born: August 11, 1902
Died: September 27, 1985

Character:
Dr. Swain

Nolan was a film and television actor. Under contract to Paramount and 20th Century Fox studios he assayed starring roles in the late 1930s and early-to-mid 1940s. Although Nolan's acting was often praised by critics he was for the most part relegated to B pictures. Despite this Nolan co-starred with a number of well-known actresses including Mae West, Dorothy McGuire, Gladys Swarthout and of course Lana Turner in Peyton Place.

TRIVIA

Goofs When Mr Rossi introduces Miss Thornton at the senior prom the audience is heard applauding a moment before they are actually seen applauding.

When the army bus taking the Peyton Place draftees away drives off, the reflection of the camera crew is briefly seen in the two last windows of the bus.

Factual Errors Mike Rossi and Dr. Swain are driving in a car and they come to a stop sign. The sign is red. All stop signs were yellow (with little round glass reflectors in the letters) in the 1940s and were not changed to red until the mid-1950s.

Interesting Facts The film received nine Oscar nominations and set a record for including four honouring supporting performances. The film failed though to win a single award.

CONTINUED

Interesting Facts

Susan Strasberg was initially set to play Allison but when she upped her salary she was fired and for a short period Debbie Reynolds was earmarked to replace her. Eventually 20 famous actresses were tested before the unknown Diane Varsi got the role.

Twentieth Century-Fox reportedly bought the film rights to Grace Metalious' novel for $100,000.

Immediately after the graduation scene there is a quick scene showing Allison MacKenzie at a typewriter. In it she is in the exact same pose seen on the back of the paperback by author Grace Metalious. The detail is exact right down to the position of her body and clothing.

The film's title was later immortalized in the lyrics to Jeannie C. Riley's 1968 hit "Harper Valley P.T.A".

Quotes

Mrs Thornton: A person doesn't always get what she deserves. Remember it. If there's anything in life you want go and get it. Don't wait for anybody to give it to you.

Gunfight at the O.K. Corral

Directed by: John Sturges - Runtime: 122 minutes

Lawman Wyatt Earp and outlaw Doc Holliday form an unlikely alliance which culminates in their participation in the legendary Gunfight at the O.K. Corral.

Gross $11,800,000

STARRING

Burton Stephen "Burt" Lancaster
Born: November 2, 1913
Died: October 20, 1994

Character:
Wyatt Earp

Film actor noted for his athletic physique, blue eyes and distinctive smile. Regarded as one of the best motion picture actors in history, Lancaster was nominated four times for Academy Awards and won once for his work in the film Elmer Gantry (1960). He also won a Golden Globe for that performance and BAFTA Awards for The Birdman of Alcatraz (1962) and Atlantic City (1980).

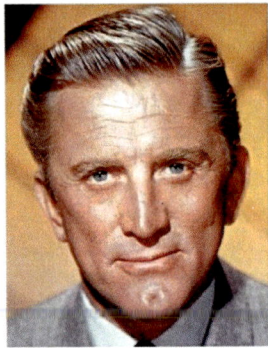

Kirk Douglas
Born: December 9, 1916

Character:
Doc Holliday

Born Issur Danielovitch, Douglas is an actor, producer, director and author. His film debut came in The Strange Love of Martha Ivers (1946) with Barbara Stanwyck. In the 1950s and 1960s, Douglas developed into a leading box-office star and during his sixty-year acting career he has appeared in over 90 movies. Douglas has received three Academy Award nominations and in 1996 received Lifetime Achievement Oscar.

Rhonda Fleming
Born: August 10, 1923

Character:
Laura Denbow

Born Marilyn Louis, Fleming is a film and television actress. She has appeared in more than forty films in total (mostly in the 1940s and 1950s) and became renowned as one of the most glamorous actresses of her day. She was nicknamed the "Queen of Technicolor" because her fair complexion and flaming red hair photographed exceptionally well in Technicolor.

TRIVIA

Goofs

When Doc Holliday is handcuffed to the bed post, Wyatt Earp throws a key to Doc but he fails to catch it. The key can be heard hitting the floor but Doc continues to unlock the handcuffs without the key.

During the gunfight a shotgun blasts holes in a wagon cover but in the next shot the holes are gone.

Factual Errors

The film has Wyatt drinking whiskey like the rest of the guys. The real Wyatt Earp was noted for his teetotal lifestyle which he rarely deviated from.

The actual gunfight at the O.K. Corral took place on the 26th October 1881 and lasted a mere 30 seconds, resulting in three dead men after an exchange of 34 bullets. The fictionalized gunfight in this movie took 4 days to film and produced an on-screen bloodbath that lasted over 5 minutes.

CONTINUED

Interesting Facts

Dennis Hopper (who plays Billy Clanton) was born and raised in Dodge City, Kansas, where Wyatt Earp was once sheriff.

This film marked Burt Lancaster's final commitment under his contract with producer Hal B. Wallis. The two never worked together again.

In his 1988 autobiography "The Ragman's Son", Kirk Douglas wrote that while playing Doc Holliday he planned exactly how many and what kinds of coughs he would have in each scene so that continuity wouldn't be a problem once the film was edited together.

Burt Lancaster doesn't sport a moustache in the film unlike the real Wyatt Earp and every other on screen portrayal of him.

Quotes

Wyatt Earp: Hold up your right hand. Do you solemnly swear to uphold... oh, this is ridiculous. You're deputized. Grab some gear, I'll get the horses.
Dr. John 'Doc' Holliday: Wait a minute, don't I get to wear a tin star?
Wyatt Earp: Not on your life!

Billy Clanton: I don't know why I get into gunfights. I guess sometimes I just get lonely.

A Farewell To Arms

Directed by: Charles Vidor - Runtime: 152 minutes

An English nurse and an American soldier on the Italian front during World War I fall in love. The horrors surrounding them test their romance to the limit.

Gross $11,000,000

STARRING

Rock Hudson
Born: November 17, 1925
Died: October 2, 1985

Character:
Lt. Frederick Henry

Hudson is generally known for his roles as a leading man in films during the 1950s and 1960s. He first achieved stardom in films such as Magnificent Obsession (1954), All That Heaven Allows (1955) and Giant (1956). Hudson later found continued success with a string of romantic comedies co-starring Doris Day. In total he starred in nearly 70 films and several television productions during a career that spanned over four decades.

Jennifer Jones
Born: March 2, 1919
Died: December 17, 2009

Character:
Catherine Barkley

Jones was an actress during the Hollywood golden years winning the Academy Award for Best Actress for her performance in The Song of Bernadette (1943). She was also nominated for Academy Awards for her performances in four other films including as Best Actress in Duel For The Sun. Jones starred in more than twenty films over a thirty-year career and in 1980 founded the Jennifer Jones Simon Foundation For Mental Health And Education.

Vittorio De Sica
Born: July 7, 1901
Died: November 13, 1974

Character:
Major Alessandro Rinaldi

An Italian director, actor and a leading figure in the neorealist movement. Four of the films he directed won Academy Awards including Sciuscià which was the first foreign film to be recognized by the Academy of Motion Picture Arts and Sciences. Another, 'Bicycle Thieves' was cited as one of the 15 most influential films in cinema history. As an actor De Sica was nominated for an Oscar for Best Supporting Actor in A Farewell to Arms.

TRIVIA

Goofs

When Hudson and Jones are in the hotel bedroom he gives her a glass of wine. The amount of wine in her glass varies between shots.

In the café, while Catherine is in hospital, Frederick is shown placing sugar cubes on a table. With three already there and his hand moving to place a fourth one, the camera cuts to a different angle and then suddenly there are five.

Interesting Facts

A large number of people left the film or were fired by producer David O. Selznick. These included; the film's original director John Huston, the unit production manager, one cinematographer, three art directors, one visual effects supervisor and all of the staff working in the villa in Rome that were hired by David O. Selznick and his wife Jennifer Jones.

CONTINUED

Interesting Facts

Selznick and Fox paid Universal $17,000 per week for Hudson's services.

Ernest Hemingway was not shy about expressing his dismay over producer David O. Selznick casting his 38-year old wife Jennifer Jones in the role of the 21-year-old nurse Catharine in the remake of his second novel, "A Farewell to Arms". Selznick had earlier tried to generate publicity for the film by making a token payment to Hemingway for the novel, even though he was not required to do so as Hemingway had already sold the rights to his book a generation before. The gesture did not earn Hemingway's goodwill.

Rock Hudson turned down Sayonara (1957) and Ben-Hur (1959) in order to make this film. He later said this was the biggest mistake of his career.

This was the second feature film adaptation of Ernest Hemingway's 1929 semi-autobiographical novel of the same name. The first film was in 1932 and starred Gary Cooper and Helen Hayes.

SPORTING WINNERS

TED WILLIAMS - MLB

ASSOCIATED PRESS - MALE ATHLETE OF THE YEAR

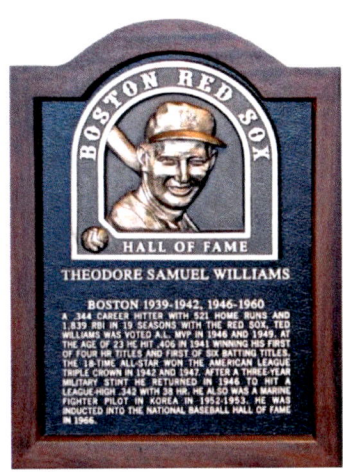  

Theodore Samuel "Ted" Williams
Born: August 30, 1918 in San Diego, California
Died: July 5, 2002 in Inverness, Florida
MLB Debut: April 20, 1939, for the Boston Red Sox
Last MLB Appearance: September 28, 1960, for the Boston Red Sox

Ted Williams was a professional baseball player and manager. He played his entire 19-year Major League Baseball career as a left fielder for the Boston Red Sox from 1939-1942 and 1946-1960. Nicknamed "The Kid", "The Splendid Splinter", "Teddy Ballgame" and "The Thumper", Williams is regarded as one of the greatest hitters in baseball history.

MLB Statistics:

Batting Average	Hits	Home Runs	Runs Batted In
.344	2,654	521	1,839

Williams was a seventeen-time All-Star, a two-time recipient of the American League Most Valuable Player Award, a six-time AL batting champion and a two-time Triple Crown winner. A left-handed batter he was known for his perfect swing and 20/10 eyesight. He would not swing at bad balls and therefore was often walked by pitchers. This talent contributed to his yet-unbroken record of bases on balls, at .482.

Williams retired from playing in 1960 and was inducted into the Baseball Hall of Fame in 1966 in his first year of eligibility. He went on to manage the Washington Senators/Texas Rangers franchise from 1969 to 1972 and his involvement in the Jimmy Fund helped raise millions of dollars for cancer care and research. In 1991 President George H. W. Bush presented Williams with the Presidential Medal of Freedom.

Althea Gibson - Tennis
Associated Press - Female Athlete of the Year

Althea Gibson
Born: August 25, 1927 in Clarendon County, South Carolina
Died: September 28, 2003 in East Orange, New Jersey

Althea Gibson was a tennis player, professional golfer and the first black athlete to cross the color line of international tennis. In 1956 she became the first person of color to win a Grand Slam title (the French Open). The following year she won both Wimbledon and the U.S. Nationals (precursor of the U.S. Open), and then won both again in 1958. For this she was voted Female Athlete of the Year by the Associated Press in both years. In all she won 11 Grand Slam tournaments. In 1971 Gibson was inducted into the International Tennis Hall of Fame and in 1980 the International Women's Sports Hall of Fame. In the early 1960s she also became the first black player to compete on the women's professional golf tour.

Grand Slam Titles:

	Singles	Doubles	Mixed Doubles
Australian Open	-	1957	-
French Open	1956	1956	-
Wimbledon	1957 / 1958	1956 / 1957 / 1958	-
U.S. Open	1957 / 1958	-	1957

At a time when racism and prejudice were widespread in sports and in society, Gibson was often compared to Jackie Robinson (who became the first African American to play in MLB in the modern era). It would be 15 years before another woman of color, Evonne Goolagong in 1971, won a Grand Slam championship and 43 years before another African-American woman, Serena Williams, won the first of her six U.S. Opens in 1999. Serena's sister Venus followed this by winning back-to-back titles at Wimbledon and the U.S. Open in 2000 and 2001, repeating Gibson's accomplishment of 1957 and 1958.

GOLF

THE MASTERS - DOUG FORD

The Masters Tournament is the first of the majors to be played each year and unlike the other major championships it is played at the same location - Augusta National Golf Club, Georgia. This was the 21st Masters Tournament to be held and Doug Ford won his second (and final major title) by three strokes to runner-up and three-time champion Sam Snead. The winners' share of the prize fund was $8,750.

U.S. OPEN - DICK MAYER

The U.S. Open Championship (established in 1895) was held June 12-15 at the Inverness Club in Toledo, Ohio. Dick Mayer defeated defending champion Cary Middlecoff in an 18-hole playoff to win his only major title. The prize fund was $30,000 with the winner's share being $7,200. This U.S. Open witnessed the debut of a 17-year-old amateur, Jack Nicklaus, who would go on to win a record-tying four Open titles and a record 18 major championships.

PGA CHAMPIONSHIP - LIONEL HEBERT

The 1957 and 39th PGA Championship was played July 17-21 at Miami Valley Golf Club in Dayton, Ohio. It was historically notable as the last PGA Championship played under the match play format. Lionel Hebert won the championship 2 & 1 over Dow Finsterwald (who went on to win the following year). The total prize fund was $42,100 and the winner's share was $8,000.

Lionel Herbert

Doug Ford

Dick Mayer

WORLD SERIES - MILWAUKEE BRAVES

Milwaukee Braves 4 - 3 New York Yankees

The 1957 World Series featured the defending champions the New York Yankees (American League) playing against the Milwaukee Braves (National League). The Braves won the Series in seven games and became the first team to win a championship after relocating (from Boston in 1953). Of the previous ten World Series the Yankees had participated in eight of them and won seven.

	Date	Score	Location	Time	Att.
1	Oct 2	Milwaukee Braves - 1 **New York Yankees - 3**	Yankee Stadium	2:10	69,476
2	Oct 3	**Milwaukee Braves - 4** New York Yankees - 2	Yankee Stadium	2:26	65,202
3	Oct 5	**New York Yankees - 12** Milwaukee Braves - 3	County Stadium	3:18	45,804
4	Oct 6	New York Yankees - 5 **Milwaukee Braves - 7**	County Stadium	2:31	45,804
5	Oct 7	New York Yankees - 0 **Milwaukee Braves - 1**	County Stadium	2:00	45,811
6	Oct 9	Milwaukee Braves - 2 **New York Yankees - 3**	Yankee Stadium	2:09	61,408
7	Oct 10	**Milwaukee Braves - 5** New York Yankees - 0	Yankee Stadium	2:34	61,207

World Series MVP: Lew Burdette (Milwaukee Braves)

Horse Racing

Gallant Man winning the 1957 Belmont Stakes by 8 lengths.

Gallant Man (March 20, 1954 - September 7, 1988) was a thoroughbred racehorse who was one of the most successful racehorses foaled outside of the United States. He is remembered equally for his loss in the 1957 Kentucky Derby as for his record breaking track and race record in the Belmont Stakes over favourite Bold Ruler (a record only beaten in 1973 by Secretariat - a horse sired by Bold Ruler). In the Kentucky Derby Gallant Man would almost certainly have won the race but his jockey, Hall of Famer Bill Shoemaker, misjudged the finish line and stood up too early in his stirrups slowing Gallant Man's rush for the wire. This error remains one of the biggest blunders in racing history.

Kentucky Derby - Iron Liege

The Kentucky Derby is held annually at Churchill Downs in Louisville, Kentucky on the first Saturday in May. The race is a Grade I stakes race for three-year-olds and is one and a quarter miles in length.

Preakness Stakes - Bold Ruler

The Preakness Stakes is held on the third Saturday in May each year at Pimlico Race Course in Baltimore, Maryland. It is a Grade I race run over a distance of 9.5 furlongs (1 3/16 miles) on dirt.

Belmont Stakes - Gallant Man

The Belmont Stakes is Grade I race held every June at Belmont Park in Elmont, New York. It is 1.5 miles in length and open to three-year-old thoroughbreds. It takes place on a Saturday between June 5 and June 11.

Football - NFL Championship

Championship Game

Detroit Lions 59-14 **Cleveland Browns**

Played: December 29, 1957 at Briggs Stadium in Detroit, Michigan.
Attendance: 55,263

The 1957 NFL season was the 38th regular season of the National Football League. The season ended with the Detroit Lions defeating the Cleveland Browns in the NFL championship game, 59-14.

Conference Results:

Eastern Conference

Team	P	W	L	T	PCT	PF	PA
Cleveland Browns	**12**	**9**	**2**	**1**	**.818**	**269**	**172**
New York Giants	12	7	5	0	.583	254	211
Pittsburgh Steelers	12	6	6	0	.500	161	178
Washington Redskins	12	5	6	1	.455	251	230
Philadelphia Eagles	12	4	8	0	.333	173	230
Chicago Cardinals	12	3	9	0	.250	200	299

Western Conference

Team	P	W	L	T	PCT	PF	PA
Detroit Lions	**12**	**8**	**4**	**0**	**.667**	**251**	**231**
San Francisco 49ers	12	8	4	0	.667	260	264
Baltimore Colts	12	7	5	0	.583	303	235
Los Angeles Rams	12	6	6	0	.500	307	278
Chicago Bears	12	5	7	0	.417	203	211
Green Bay Packers	12	3	9	0	.250	218	311

P= Games Played, W = Wins, L = Losses, T = Ties,
PCT= Winning Percentage, PF= Points For, PA = Points Against

Most Valuable Player: Jim Brown - Running Back - Cleveland Browns

Coach of the Year: George Wilson - Detroit Lions

Basketball - NBA Finals

4 - 3

Boston Celtics   St. Louis Hawks

Series Summary

	Date	Home Team	Result	Road Team
1	March 30	Boston Celtics	123-125 (2OT)	**St. Louis Hawks**
2	March 31	**Boston Celtics**	119-99	St. Louis Hawks
3	April 6	**St. Louis Hawks**	100-98	Boston Celtics
4	April 7	St. Louis Hawks	118-123	**Boston Celtics**
5	April 9	**Boston Celtics**	124-109	St. Louis Hawks
6	April 11	**St. Louis Hawks**	96-94	Boston Celtics
7	April 13	**Boston Celtics**	125-123 (2OT)	St. Louis Hawks

The 1957 World Championship Series was the conclusion of the NBA 1956-57 season. The Eastern Conference champion, the Boston Celtics, faced the Western Conference champion, the St. Louis Hawks, in a best-of-seven series that the Celtics won 4 games to 3. This was the first trip to the Finals for both team and would be the first of 17 NBA titles for the Boston Celtics.

Boston Marathon

John J. Kelley

The Boston Marathon is the oldest annual marathon in the world and dates back to 1897.

Race result:

1. **John J. Kelley (USA)**   **2:20:05**
2. Veikko Karvonen (FIN)   2:23:54
3. Chiang W. Lim (KOR)   2:24:59

NHL Finals - Stanley Cup

4 - 1

Montreal Canadiens   Boston Bruins

Series Summary:

	Date	Home Team	Result	Road Team
1	April 6	**Montreal Canadiens**	5-1	Boston Bruins
2	April 9	**Montreal Canadiens**	1-0	Boston Bruins
3	April 11	Boston Bruins	2-4	**Montreal Canadiens**
4	April 14	**Boston Bruins**	2-0	Montreal Canadiens
5	April 16	**Montreal Canadiens**	5-1	Boston Bruins

The 1957 Stanley Cup Final NHL championship series was contested by the defending champions the Montreal Canadiens and the Boston Bruins. The Canadiens, making their seventh consecutive Final appearance, beat the Boston Bruins 4-1 for their second straight Cup victory.

Indianapolis 500
Sam Hanks

The 41st International 500-Mile Sweepstakes Race was held at the Indianapolis Motor Speedway on Thursday, May 30, 1957. Sam Hanks won this at his thirteenth attempt and received a record $103,844 purse - the first driver to win a $100,000 single-race payday (the total race purse was also a record at over $300,000). Hanks won the race in George Salih's "Lay-down Offy". The Offenhauser engine was mounted on its side and shifted off-center. This was done in order to lower the center of gravity, reduce frontal area and counterbalance the body roll in the turns. The car that Hanks drove for the win in 1957 would win back-to-back Indy 500s with Jimmy Bryan piloting the very same chassis to victory again in 1958. This event was part of the 1957 USAC National Championship Trail and was included in the 1957 World Drivers Championship.

Tennis - U.S. National Championships

Mens Singles Champion - Malcolm Anderson - Australia
Ladies Singles Champion - Althea Gibson - U.S.

The 1957 U.S. National Championships (now known as the U.S. Open) took place on the outdoor grass courts at the West Side Tennis Club, Forest Hills in New York. The tournament ran from August 30 until September 8. It was the 77th staging of the U.S. National Championships and the fourth Grand Slam tennis event of the year.

Men's Singles Final:

Country	Player	Set 1	Set 2	Set 3
Australia	Malcolm Anderson	10	7	6
Australia	Ashley Cooper	8	5	4

Women's Singles Final:

Country	Player	Set 1	Set 2
U.S.	Althea Gibson	6	6
U.S.	Louise Brough Clapp	3	2

Men's Doubles Final:

Country	Players	Set 1	Set 2	Set 3	Set 4
Australia	Ashley Cooper / Neale Fraser	4	6	9	6
U.S.	Gardnar Mulloy / Budge Patty	6	3	7	3

Women's Doubles Final:

Country	Players	Set 1	Set 2
U.S.	Louise Brough / Margaret Osborne	6	7
U.S.	Althea Gibson / Darlene Hard	2	5

Mixed Doubles Final:

Country	Players	Set 1	Set 2
U.S. / Denmark	Althea Gibson / Kurt Nielsen	6	9
U.S. / Australia	Darlene Hard / Australia Bob Howe	3	7

THE COST OF LIVING
COMPARISON CHART

	Average Cost 1957	1957 Price Today (Including Inflation)	Average Cost 2016
House	$17,300	$147,303	$281,800
Annual Income	$2,075	$17,668	$48,187
Car	$2,650	$22,564	$33,560
Gallon of Gasoline	30¢	$2.55	$2.68
Gallon of Milk	37¢	$3.15	$3.86
DC Comic Book	10¢	$0.85	$3.99

GROCERIES

Wonder Bread (1½lb loaf)	25¢
Piggly Wiggly's Grade A Eggs (per dozen)	49¢
Chee-Zip Cheese Spread (16oz jar)	52¢
Bama Smooth Peanut Butter	47¢
Jane Parker Glazed Donuts (pkg. of 12)	29¢
Dixie Belle Saltine Crackers (1lb box)	23¢
U.S. No.1 Potatoes (per lb)	5¢
Sunkist Naval Oranges (per lb)	15¢
Rome Beauty Apples (per lb)	13¢
Del Monte Sweet Peas (can)	19¢
Skinner's Spaghetti (2x 7oz pkg.)	25¢
Swifts Premium Picnic Hams	39¢
Prime Rib Roast (per lb)	65¢
Premium Aged Sirloin Steak	69¢
Heart Of Texas Fryers (per lb)	38¢
Libby's Corned Beef (12oz can)	45¢
Captains Choice Fish Sticks (14oz pkg.)	45¢
Santa Rosa Sliced Pineapple (can)	23¢
Heinz Baby Foods (jar)	10¢
Minute Maid Lemonade (2x 6oz cans)	29¢
Maryland Club Coffee (1lb can)	$1.03
Prell Liquid Shampoo (1½oz bottle)	30¢
Colgate Aerosol Florient Deodorant (5½oz can)	89¢
Palmolive Soap (2 bars)	17¢
Zee Colored Toilet Tissue (4 rolls)	35¢
Gleem Toothpaste (large tube)	49¢
Listerine	79¢
Tide Detergent (giant box)	59¢

MISS SUNBEAM
Symbol of America's Finest Baked Foods

For Real Miracle Meals...

Miracle meals start with Sunbeam Bread. Serve it as part of a meal, or as a good companion to one. When you're shopping... look for Miss Sunbeam. To thousands of American families, she's as familiar and dear as the little girl next door.

Miss Sunbeam's picture on every loaf of Sunbeam Bread, every package of Sunbeam Rolls, is your best guarantee of freshness and quality. Look for her... when you plan your miracle meals, and take plenty of Sunbeam home to your family.

Reach For **Sunbeam** Bread, Rolls and Buns

Who made tomato flavor come alive in catsup?

Del Monte chefs did... with pineapple distilled vinegar! Rich-ripe tomato flavor is the life of the party in this catsup! Del Monte's own exciting pineapple distilled vinegar is the reason. It does such a great blending job, the superb tomatoes and zesty spices in Del Monte Catsup just naturally put out more flavor. Why not give a special lift to everything from the most high-falutin' hors d'oeuvre to the humblest hamburger? Try Del Monte Brand Catsup.

Party time is Planters Peanut time!

Something wonderful happens to a party when you bring in the Planters Peanuts! Suddenly, every drink seems to taste better... every guest seems to be having more fun. These big, plump, party-perfect peanuts are America's favorite snack. Easy to serve, too! Just open the vacuum can and out pop crisp, crunchy, roaster-fresh Planters Peanuts.

© Mr. Peanut

PLANTERS IS THE WORD FOR PEANUTS

CLOTHES

Women's Clothing		Men's Clothing	
Ladies Winter Coat	$16	Tweed Topcoat	$28.75
Nelly Don Coat Dress	$17.95	Sports Coat	$24.50
Women's Suits	$17.75	Motorcycle Jacket	$8.77
Fall Dress	$6	Brookfield Gabardine Suit	$19.75
Winter Skirt	$2.77	Wool Slacks	$12.95
Vanity Fair Petticoat	$2.95	Pullover Sleeveless Sweater	$4.95
Peter Pan Bra	$3.98	Sport Shirt	$1.88
Nylonized Tricot Panties	29¢	Flannel Shirts	$1
Shoes - Ivy League Casuals	$5.95	Penney's PJ's	$2.44
Shoes - Suede Flats	$2	Engineer Boots	$9.95

TOYS

Heavy Duty Velocipedes	$7.95
Happi-Time Pedal Drive Auto	$13.88
Ride 'em Stick	$2.99
10½in Walking Black Bear With Xylophone	$1.98
Western Marshal Set With Badge	$4.95
21in Doll Carriage	$5.39
Cindy Doll	$3.98
Animal Soft Toy	$2.98
7in Radar Siren Jeep	98¢
Official Basketball Set	$7.98
JC Higgins Beginners Roller Skates	$1.98
Split Cowhide Football	$2.98
Toy Town Cook And Bake Set	$1.98
Slinky Dog	$2

Insist on **Slinky** Toys

AT YOUR NEAREST TOY COUNTER

JAMES INDUSTRIES, PAOLI, PA.

SLINKY WORM • SLINKY TRAIN • SLINKY JUNIOR • SLINKY EYES • SLINKY BUCKO

ELECTRICAL ITEMS

Admiral T23A2 Embassy 21in B&W TV	$229.95
RCA Victor Portable TV (36sq inch viewing area)	$79.95
Coldspot 15 Cubic Foot Freezer	$278
Maytag Washer	$149.95
Symphonic Hi-Fi Portable Record Player	$79.95
Electra Tape Hi-Fi Recorder	$99.95
GE Steam Iron	$12.95
Kenmore Portable Mixer	$12.95
Automatic Toaster	$18.95
Quality Electric Blanket	$12.87
GE Clock Radio	$26.95

YOU HAVE NEVER SEEN TABLE TV LIKE THIS!

Big 155-Square-Inch Picture!   *Most Slender of All!*   *Even the Back Is Beautiful!*

NEW *Slender Seventeener* BY PHILCO

Goes anywhere in the house beautifully!

Go ahead — put a Philco Slender Seventeener on your coffee table, room divider, *anywhere* in *any* room. This new Philco is fashion-styled to look stunning from every angle. It's the most compact, powerful, big screen table TV ever! And so easy to carry, it's like having TV in every room!

Slender Seventeeners have a new long-life transformer development, the Philco Germanitron.

New advanced 110° picture tube. All top controls. Powerful built-in antenna. Cabinets come in rich mahogany and blond finishes, as well as gorgeous new colors like peacock blue and charcoal!

Yes, everything about the new Philco Slender Seventeener is new and exciting! See them now at your Philco dealer's. You'll want to own one—and you can for as little as **$159.95**

PRICES SUBJECT TO CHANGE. SLIGHTLY HIGHER SOUTH OR WEST

LOOK AHEAD... *and you'll choose* **PHILCO.**

OTHER ITEMS

Goodyear Tyres (from)	$13.95
Goodyear 6 Volt Car Battery	$8.95
Lone Star Automatic Gas Clothes Dryer	$179.95
Dason 'Teen-Age' Genuine Diamond Ring	$19.95
Stratolounger Special World's Most Comfortable Chair	$79.50
Serta-Lux Smooth Top Mattress	$44
21in Weekend Suitcase	$11.95
Cedar Hope Chest	$49.95
Travel Alarm Clock	$4.95

Soaring tail fins dramatize the low sweeping lines of the Dodge Custom Royal. New wide-scope windshield, clean-contoured grille and dashing "twin-lights" accent its new shape of motion, too.

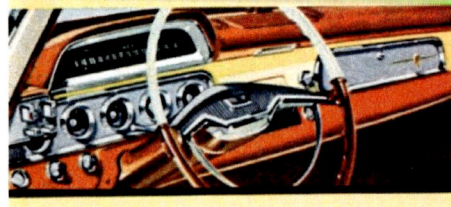

Completely new push-button 3-speed Torque-Flite automatic transmission is standard on every Dodge Custom Royal. Now—just push the "N" button to start the engine, the "D" button to go.

FIRST SHOWING!

Dodge CUSTOM Royal

ALL NEW FOR 1957!

★ New Torque-Flite push-button go! ★ New low look!
★ New Torsion-Aire ride! ★ New Total-Contact brakes!
★ New safety-strength design! ★ New simpler starting!
★ More fine-car features than any other car at its price!

Now see the new queen of automotive fashion... the long, low, lovely Dodge Custom Royal for '57! Drive and ride in the all-new luxury of the biggest, finest Dodge of all. It's on display now at your Dodge-DeSoto dealer's.

You're always a step ahead in the cars of the Forward Look ➤

U.S. Coins

Official Circulated U.S. Coins		Years Produced
Half-Cent	½¢	1792 - 1857
Cent (Penny)	1¢	1793 - Present
2-Cent	2¢	1864 - 1873
3-Cent	3¢	1851 - 1889
Half-Dime	5¢	1792 - 1873
Five Cent Nickel	5¢	1866 - Present
Dime	10¢	1792 - Present
20-Cent	20¢	1875 - 1878
Quarter	25¢	1796 - Present
Half Dollar	50¢	1794 - Present
Dollar Coin	$1	1794 - Present
Quarter Eagle	$2.50	1792 - 1929
Three-Dollar Piece	$3	1854 - 1889
Four-Dollar Piece	$4	1879 - 1880
Half Eagle	$5	1795 – 1929
Commemorative Half Eagle	$5	1980 - Present
Silver Eagle	$1	1986 - Present
Gold Eagle	$5	1986 - Present
Platinum Eagle	$10 - $100	1997 - Present
Double Eagle (Gold)	$20	1849 - 1933
Half Union	$50	1915

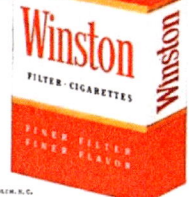